HALKIDIKI
TRAVEL GUIDE 2024

A Comprehensive Pocket Guide for an Enchanting Travel Experience with Insider's Tips, Must-Visit Attractions, Budget-Friendly Activities and Itineraries

STELLA MELISSA

Halkidiki Travel Guide 2024...

Copyright © 2023, Stella Melissa

All rights reserved. No part of this publication may be reproduced, distributed, or transmitted in any form or by any means, including photocopying, recording, or other electronic or mechanical methods, without the prior written permission of the publisher, except in the case of brief quotations embodied in critical reviews and certain other noncommercial uses permitted by copyright law.

Halkidiki Travel Guide 2024...

TABLE OF CONTENTS

INTRODUCTION

CHAPTER 1:

Introduction to Halkidiki

- Halkidiki: Quick Facts and Statistics
- Brief History of Chalkidiki
- Geography and Climate
- Getting to Halkidiki
- Local Transportation

CHAPTER 2:

Planning Your Halkidiki Adventure

- Choosing the Right Time to Visit
- Setting Your Budget
- Accommodation Options
- Creating an Itinerary
- Travel Essentials and Packing Tips

CHAPTER 3:

Discovering Halkidiki's Regions
- Kassandra Peninsula
- Sithonia Peninsula
- Mount Athos Peninsula

CHAPTER 4:

Must-See Attractions in Halkidiki
- Ancient Olynthus
- Petralona Cave
- Athos Monastic Community
- Nikiti Old Village
- Sani Resort and Marina
- Turtle Lake

CHAPTER 5:

Embracing Halkidiki's Rich Culture
- Halkidiki's Gastronomy Delights
- Traditional Chalkidian Cuisine

- Festivals and Celebrations
- Folklore and Artisan Crafts
- Local Music and Dance

CHAPTER 6:
Outdoor Adventures and Recreational Activities
- Hiking in Halkidiki's Forests
- Watersports and Beach Activities
- Cruising the Aegean Sea
- Bird Watching in Axios Delta National Park
- Golfing in Halkidiki
- Day Trips to Nearby Islands

CHAPTER 7:
Halkidiki for All Travelers
- Family-Friendly Experiences
- Romantic Escapes for Couples
- Seniors' Relaxation Retreats
- Halkidiki for Students

- Solo Traveler's Guide and Safety Tips

CHAPTER 8:

Practical Information and Resources
- Currency and Money Matters
- Language and Communication
- Health and Safety Guidelines
- Sustainable Travel in Halkidiki
- Emergency Contacts and Useful Information

APPENDIX I:

Essential Travel Resources for Halkidiki
- Greek Phrases for Travelers with Pronunciation Guide
- Recommended Travel Apps
- Other Useful Information

APPENDIX II:
- Map of Halkidiki

Halkidiki Travel Guide 2024...

"

Remember that happiness is a way of travel – not a destination.

-Roy M. Goodman

"

Halkidiki Travel Guide 2024...

INTRODUCTION

Dear Adventurer, buckle up, for I'm about to whisk you away on a journey that reads like a dream and feels like a love affair with a Greek paradise. Welcome to "Halkidiki Travel Guide 2024," a book that's not just about travel; it's an enchanted portal to a world where myths become memories and where the beauty of the Aegean embraces you like an old friend.

My own journey to Halkidiki was serendipitous, a whisper from the universe that there's a place where your senses awaken with each wave that caresses the shore, where the sunsets blaze like a bonfire in the sky, and where time feels suspended in the embrace of Greece's hidden gem.

Halkidiki is a land of secrets, where each of its "fingers" tells a unique story. Kassandra, the enchantress of the west, lured me in with her sun-drenched beaches and crystal-clear waters. It's the kind of place where the sea sings lullabies, and the aroma of souvlaki dances on the breeze. There, I discovered that happiness tastes like the first bite of a ripe, juicy peach.

Venturing to Sithonia, the central finger, was like stepping into a postcard. Pine-scented forests meet secluded coves where the sea shimmers with all the shades of blue you can imagine. Nature reigns supreme here, and you'll find yourself sharing the beach with the whispering pines and the occasional seagull. It's a land of reflection, where I found solace in simplicity.

And then there's Mount Athos, the mystical eastern finger. It's a world unto itself, where time bows to tradition, and monasteries perch on cliffs like wise old sages. The monks, whose faces hold the secrets of centuries, opened their doors to reveal a world where faith and history intertwine in a dance of devotion.

But Halkidiki isn't just a feast for the eyes; it's a culinary delight. Each meal is a symphony of flavors, a celebration of olives, olive oil, fresh seafood, and herbs that perfume the air. As I savored each bite of grilled octopus and spoonful of moussaka, I realized that this is where your taste buds go to find true love.

My journey also led me to charming villages where time is an ally, not an adversary. There, I met locals who became friends, sharing stories that are as old as the hills and as warm as the Mediterranean sun. It was in these moments that I uncovered the heart of Halkidiki.

So, as you turn the pages of "Halkidiki Travel Guide 2024," remember that you're not just reading a book; you're embarking on a love affair with a destination that is as diverse as it is dazzling. Whether you're a sunseeker, an explorer, a history buff, or a gastronome, Halkidiki has a tale to tell and an adventure to offer.

This isn't a travel guide; it's a voyage through the heart of Halkidiki. It's an invitation to uncover hidden gems, to dive into turquoise waters, and to savor the taste of Greece. It's an ode to a place where myths become memories, and where each sunrise brings the promise of new wonders.

Are you ready to fall in love with Halkidiki? The adventure begins here.

Halkidiki Travel Guide 2024...

CHAPTER 1:

Introduction to Halkidiki

Halkidiki, also known as Chalkidiki, is a Greek peninsula with a captivating blend of natural beauty, rich history, and vibrant culture. Situated in the northern part of Greece, Halkidiki is a destination that has something for everyone, from pristine beaches and lush forests to ancient ruins and charming villages. In this chapter, we will delve into the essentials of Halkidiki, providing quick facts and statistics, a brief historical overview, insights into the region's geography and climate, tips on how to get to Halkidiki, and an exploration of local transportation options.

Halkidiki: Quick Facts and Statistics

- Location: Halkidiki is a peninsula in Greece's northern region. It reaches the Aegean Sea and is distinguished by its three-pronged shape, with three major "legs" thrusting out into the water.

- Economy: The economy of Halkidiki is predominantly driven by tourism, agriculture, and fishing. Tourism plays a crucial role, with visitors drawn to the region's stunning beaches, historic sites, and natural beauty.

- Time Zone: Halkidiki operates on Eastern European Time (EET), which is UTC+2, and observes daylight saving time during the summer months, shifting to Eastern European Summer Time (EEST), which is UTC+3.

- Education: Halkidiki has several educational institutions, including primary and secondary schools, as well as vocational training centers. Additionally, students can pursue higher education in nearby cities.

- Government: Halkidiki is administratively divided into multiple municipalities and communities, each with its own local government. These local governments operate under the framework of the Greek legal and political system.

Brief History of Chalkidiki

The history of Halkidiki is a tapestry woven with threads of ancient civilizations, conquests, and cultural exchanges. This region has a rich and diverse historical background:

- Ancient Times: Halkidiki was inhabited by various ancient Greek tribes, including the Macedonians. The peninsula was part of the wider Greek world and played a role in the Hellenistic period.

- Roman and Byzantine Eras: During the Roman period, Halkidiki was under Roman rule and saw the construction of important structures, such as the ancient city of Olynthus. In the Byzantine era, the region was dotted with monasteries and religious sites.

- Ottoman Rule: In the 14th century, Halkidiki fell under Ottoman rule, which lasted for several centuries. The Ottomans left their mark on the region, influencing its culture and architecture.

- Greek Independence: Halkidiki, like the rest of Greece, played a part in the Greek War of Independence in the early 19th century. The region eventually became part of the modern Greek state.

Geography and Climate

Halkidiki's geography is characterized by its unique three-pronged shape, each "leg" offering a distinct landscape and character:

- Kassandra (Kassándra): The westernmost "leg" of Halkidiki, Kassandra is known for its lively coastal towns, sandy beaches, and a bustling nightlife. Its terrain is relatively flat, making it ideal for leisurely walks and water sports.

- Sithonia (Síthonia): The central "leg" of Halkidiki, Sithonia boasts a more rugged and natural landscape. It is renowned for its pristine beaches, charming villages, and a relaxed atmosphere.

- Athos (Áthos): The easternmost "leg" is known as the Athos Peninsula. It is home to the monastic community of Mount Athos, a UNESCO World Heritage site. Access to this region is restricted to males, and it is famous for its spiritual and natural significance.

Halkidiki enjoys a Mediterranean climate, characterized by hot, dry summers and mild, wet winters. Summers are the peak tourist season, with temperatures often reaching into the 30s°C (80s-90s°F). Winters are milder, with temperatures rarely falling below freezing. The region's climate is ideal for both beachgoers and nature enthusiasts.

Getting to Halkidiki

Reaching Halkidiki is relatively straightforward, with several transportation options available:

- By Air: Thessaloniki International Airport "Macedonia" (SKG) is the nearest major airport to Halkidiki. Located about 45 minutes away by road, the airport serves both domestic and international flights. From the airport, you can rent a car, take a taxi, or use public transportation to reach Halkidiki.

- By Road: If you're traveling from Thessaloniki or other parts of Greece, you can access Halkidiki by road. The road network is well-maintained, and there are bus services connecting Halkidiki with Thessaloniki and other cities.

- By Sea: Halkidiki has several ports, including the port of Thessaloniki, which welcomes ferries and cruise ships. If you're island-hopping or arriving from nearby destinations, traveling by sea can be a scenic and enjoyable option.

- By Public Transportation: Public buses operate from Thessaloniki to various destinations in Halkidiki. These buses provide an affordable and convenient way to explore the region.

Local Transportation

Getting around Halkidiki and exploring its diverse "legs" requires an efficient local transportation system:

- Buses: Local buses connect Halkidiki's towns, villages, and beaches. They are a cost-effective way to explore the region. You can find schedules and routes at bus stations and online.

- Taxis: Taxis are readily available in Halkidiki, providing a convenient mode of transportation, especially for short journeys or when you prefer private travel.

- Car Rentals: Renting a car is a popular choice for visitors who want to explore Halkidiki at their own pace. Many rental agencies can be found at the airport and in major towns.

- Boats: In Sithonia and Athos, boat tours and water taxis are common ways to access secluded beaches, islands, and monastic sites.

Halkidiki's transportation options make it easy to explore the region's diverse landscapes and cultural sites. Whether you prefer leisurely bus rides, the freedom of a rental car, or the adventure of a boat tour, Halkidiki's local transportation caters to various travel styles.

Halkidiki beckons with its stunning beaches, historic treasures, and welcoming atmosphere. As we continue our journey through this guide, we'll explore the distinct charms of each "leg" of Halkidiki, uncovering hidden gems and unforgettable experiences in this Greek paradise.

Halkidiki Travel Guide 2024...

CHAPTER 2:

Planning Your Halkidiki Adventure

Welcome to the exciting phase of planning your adventure in Halkidiki. In this chapter, we'll guide you through the various aspects of preparing for your journey to this captivating Greek peninsula. We'll discuss choosing the right time to visit, setting your budget, exploring accommodation options, creating a fascinating itinerary, and providing essential travel tips for a memorable Halkidiki experience.

Choosing the Right Time to Visit

Selecting the best time to visit Halkidiki is a critical first step in planning your adventure. The region experiences distinct seasons, each offering unique experiences:

- Summer (June to August): Summer is the high tourist season in Halkidiki, with warm and sunny weather. It's the ideal time for beach enthusiasts, water sports, and lively nightlife. The sea is warm and inviting, making it perfect for swimming and snorkeling. Expect higher prices and crowded beaches during this period.

- Spring (April to May): Spring brings milder weather and blooming landscapes. It's an excellent time for nature lovers and hikers, as the countryside is adorned with wildflowers. The sea may still be a bit chilly for swimming, but it's a great season for exploring historic sites and hiking trails.

- Autumn (September to October): Autumn offers pleasant weather, with warm days and cooler nights. The sea remains inviting for swimming, and the crowds begin to thin out. It's a wonderful time for those seeking a more relaxed and budget-friendly experience.

- Winter (November to March): Halkidiki is less crowded in winter, making it an attractive option for travelers who enjoy a quieter and more authentic experience. While swimming might not be on the agenda, you can explore local culture, dine at cozy tavernas, and enjoy the serene beauty of the region.

Your choice of timing depends on your preferences and the experiences you seek. Consider your interests and whether you prefer a bustling summer atmosphere or a tranquil, off-season escape.

Setting Your Budget

Setting a budget is an essential part of planning your Halkidiki adventure. To help you plan, let's explore different budget levels and provide rough estimates for each:

- Budget Traveler (€30-€50 per day): Budget travelers can enjoy a comfortable experience in Halkidiki. Stay in hostels, guesthouses, or budget hotels, and dine at local tavernas. Public transportation and occasional splurges on tours or activities are manageable within this budget.

- Mid-Range Traveler (€70-€150 per day): Mid-range travelers can have a more relaxed experience with a higher budget. Choose from mid-range hotels or boutique accommodations, dine at a mix of local restaurants and upscale options, and participate in various activities such as boat tours and guided excursions.

- Luxury Traveler (€200 and above per day): Luxury travelers can indulge in the finest Halkidiki has to offer. Stay in upscale resorts or villas, savor gourmet cuisine at high-end restaurants, and enjoy private tours, spa treatments, and other premium services.

These budget estimates cover accommodation, food, transportation, and some activities. Keep in mind that prices can vary depending on the specific location within Halkidiki, so it's wise to research and plan accordingly. Additionally, consider setting aside some extra funds for unexpected expenses and souvenirs.

Accommodation Options

Halkidiki offers a wide range of accommodation options to suit every taste and budget. Here are some samples of accommodation choices, complete with their updated contact information:

1. Ekies All Senses Resort (Vourvourou, Sithonia)

- Description: This luxury boutique hotel is nestled in a picturesque bay, offering stylish rooms, a tranquil atmosphere, and stunning sea views. It's an excellent choice for couples and travelers seeking a peaceful retreat.

- Website: www.ekies.gr
- Contact: info@ekies.gr
- Phone: +30 2375 091146

2. Hotel Ammon Zeus (Kallithea, Kassandra)

- Description: Hotel Ammon Zeus is a four-star beachfront hotel, perfect for families and travelers who enjoy the vibrant atmosphere of Kallithea. It features comfortable rooms, multiple dining options, and direct access to the beach.
-Website: www.hotelammonzeus.gr

- Contact: info@hotelammonzeus.gr
- Phone: +30 23510 32761

3. Meli Palace (Polygyros, Central Halkidiki)

- Description: Meli Palace is an all-inclusive resort offering a range of amenities for families and couples. With multiple pools, restaurants, and entertainment options, it's a great choice for those who want everything at their fingertips.

-Website: www.melipalace.com
- Contact: info@melipalace.com
- Phone: +30 23730 92180

4. Akti-S Ouranoupoli (Ouranoupoli, Athos)
- Description: This family-run guesthouse offers cozy rooms and a warm, welcoming atmosphere. It's situated

in the charming village of Ouranoupoli, making it an excellent choice for those interested in exploring Mount Athos.

- Website: www.akti-s.gr
- Contact: info@akti-s.gr
- Phone: +30 23770 71103

These are just a few examples of the diverse accommodation options in Halkidiki. When selecting your accommodation, consider your preferences, budget, and the location you wish to explore.

Creating an Itinerary

Now, let's embark on the exciting task of creating your Halkidiki itinerary. This region offers a wide array of attractions and activities, catering to a variety of interests:

Day 1: Arrival and Beach Time
 - Arrive in Halkidiki and settle into your chosen accommodation.
 - Head to the nearest beach to relax and soak in the Mediterranean sunshine.

Day 2: Explore Kassandra
 - Visit the village of Afytos for a taste of traditional Greek charm.
 - Explore the Kassandra Peninsula's western coast, known for its lively nightlife and beautiful beaches.

Day 3: Sithonia's Natural Beauty

- Journey to Sithonia and enjoy the pristine beaches on its eastern coast.

- Discover the lush greenery and serene atmosphere of the Sithonia Peninsula.

Day 4: Cultural Encounters

- Explore the town of Nikiti and visit the Church of St. Nikitas.

- Take a guided tour of the Petralona Cave, known for its impressive stalactites and stalagmites.

Day 5: Athos Peninsula and Mount Athos

- Take a boat tour around the Athos Peninsula, viewing the monasteries from the sea.

- Explore Ouranoupoli and its charming streets, ending your day with a delicious seafood dinner.

Day 6: Ancient Olynthus and Archaeological Wonders

- Visit the ancient city of Olynthus, an archaeological site with well-preserved ruins.

- Explore the ancient village of Stagira, the birthplace of Aristotle.

Day 7: Departure

- Depending on your departure time, spend your last moments in Halkidiki at the beach or shopping for souvenirs.

- Bid farewell to this enchanting peninsula and head to the airport or your next destination.

This sample itinerary provides a mix of relaxation, cultural exploration, and outdoor activities. Feel free to adjust it according to your interests and the duration of your stay.

Travel Essentials and Packing Tips

To ensure a smooth and enjoyable adventure in Halkidiki, consider the following travel essentials and packing tips:

- Travel Documents: Ensure your passport, visa (if required), and any necessary travel permits are up to date. Make copies of these documents and store them separately.

- Currency: The official currency in Greece is the Euro (€). Have some cash on hand for small expenses, and inform your bank about your travel plans to avoid any issues with your credit or debit card.

- Electrical Adapters: Greece uses Type C and Type F electrical outlets. If your devices have different plug types, bring the necessary adapters.
- Language: While English is widely spoken in tourist areas, learning a few basic Greek phrases can enhance your experience and make a positive impression on locals.

- Sun Protection: Halkidiki enjoys a sunny climate. Pack sunscreen, sunglasses, and a wide-brimmed hat to protect yourself from the sun's rays.

- Beach Gear: If you plan to spend time on the beaches, bring beach towels, swimwear, and beach footwear.

- Comfortable Shoes: Walking shoes or sandals with good arch support are essential for exploring the region's streets and trails.

- Medications: If you take prescription medications, ensure you have an adequate supply for your trip, along with any necessary medical documents.

- Travel Insurance: Consider purchasing comprehensive travel insurance to cover unexpected events such as trip cancellations, medical emergencies, and lost luggage.

- Reusable Water Bottle: Carry a reusable water bottle to stay hydrated. Tap water in Halkidiki is generally safe to drink.

- Local Maps and Guidebooks: Even in the digital age, physical maps and guidebooks can be helpful for navigating the region.

- Daypack: A small daypack is useful for carrying essentials during day trips and explorations.

With these travel essentials and packing tips, you'll be well-prepared for your Halkidiki adventure, ensuring a memorable and hassle-free experience.

As you plan your adventure, remember that Halkidiki is a region of diverse landscapes, from sun-kissed beaches to lush forests and ancient ruins. The journey ahead promises enchanting discoveries and cherished memories, and we'll continue to unravel the secrets of Halkidiki in the chapters to come.

CHAPTER 3:

Discovering Halkidiki's Regions

Halkidiki, or Chalkidiki, is a land of contrasts, where each of its three peninsulas offers a unique and captivating experience. In this chapter, we will explore the history, attractions, and dining options of the following regions:

1. Kassandra Peninsula: Sun, Sand, and Beaches
2. Sithonia Peninsula: Nature and Serenity
3. Mount Athos Peninsula: Spiritual and Cultural Exploration

Kassandra Peninsula

- History: The Kassandra Peninsula, the westernmost "leg" of Halkidiki, is known for its vibrant atmosphere and beautiful coastline. In antiquity, this region was a part of ancient Macedonia and later a Roman province. Today, it's a hub for tourism, with numerous resorts, cafes, and lively nightlife.

- Attractions: Kassandra is famous for its long stretches of sandy beaches lapped by the azure waters of the Aegean Sea. You can explore the picturesque village of Afytos, characterized by its cobblestone streets, stone houses, and a stunning view of the sea from its rocky cliffs. Don't miss the chance to visit the Sani Resort, which offers a range of dining, shopping, and entertainment options, as well as a beautiful marina.

- Dining Options: Kassandra boasts a diverse culinary scene. You can savor fresh seafood at seaside tavernas or sample Greek and international dishes at upscale restaurants. Be sure to try local specialties like grilled octopus, moussaka, and souvlaki. Enjoy a glass of Greek wine and experience traditional Greek hospitality in the village's numerous cafes.

Sithonia Peninsula

- History: Sithonia, the central "leg" of Halkidiki, is characterized by its natural beauty and rugged landscapes. Historically, this region was known for its dense forests and served as a source of timber for shipbuilding during ancient times. Today, Sithonia remains a haven for those seeking tranquility and natural serenity.

- Attractions: Sithonia's coastline is dotted with pristine, unspoiled beaches that are perfect for relaxation and water sports. Explore the charming villages of Nikiti and Neos Marmaras, each offering a taste of authentic Greek life. Nature enthusiasts can hike through the verdant hills and forests, discovering hidden lakes and lush landscapes.

- Dining Options: Sithonia is an excellent place to experience authentic Greek cuisine in a peaceful setting. Many traditional tavernas and family-run restaurants offer a taste of local dishes prepared with fresh ingredients. Enjoy traditional Greek salads, grilled fish, and hearty stews while surrounded by the beauty of Sithonia's natural landscapes.

Mount Athos Peninsula

- History: The easternmost "leg" of Halkidiki is the Mount Athos Peninsula, home to the monastic community of Mount Athos. This region's history is deeply intertwined with religion and spirituality, dating back to the Byzantine era.

- Attractions: Mount Athos is renowned for its monastic communities, with many monasteries dating back to the Middle Ages. While access to the monastic area is restricted to males, you can still take boat tours around the peninsula to view the monasteries from the sea. Explore the village of Ouranoupoli, where you can visit the Tower of Ouranoupolis and enjoy fresh seafood at waterfront restaurants.

- Dining Options: Dining in Mount Athos is a unique experience. The village of Ouranoupoli offers a selection of tavernas that serve fresh seafood, traditional Greek dishes, and local delicacies. Try dishes like octopus in wine sauce, fresh mussels, and baklava for dessert. Dining with a view of the sea and the peninsula's lush greenery is a memorable experience.

Each of these Halkidiki regions offers a distinctive experience, from sun-soaked beaches and vibrant nightlife on Kassandra to the natural beauty and serenity of Sithonia, and the spiritual and cultural exploration of the Mount Athos Peninsula. As you explore these diverse "legs" of Halkidiki, you'll uncover the rich tapestry of history, stunning landscapes, and delicious cuisine that this Greek paradise has to offer.

CHAPTER 4:

Must-See Attractions in Halkidiki

Halkidiki is a treasure trove of historical sites, natural wonders, and cultural landmarks. In this chapter, we will explore the must-see attractions of the region, delving into their history, locations, and visiting hours:

1. Ancient Olynthus

2. Petralona Cave

3. Athos Monastic Community

4. Nikiti Old Village

5. Sani Resort and Marina

6. Turtle Lake

Ancient Olynthus

- History: Ancient Olynthus was an ancient Greek city located in the region of Chalkidiki. Founded in the 5th century BC, it thrived as a prosperous city until its destruction by Philip II of Macedon in 348 BC. Olynthus was known for its well-preserved city layout, which offered valuable insights into ancient urban planning.

- Location: The archaeological site of Ancient Olynthus is situated near the modern village of Olynthos in Chalkidiki. It's approximately 3 kilometers west of Moudania and about 80 kilometers southeast of Thessaloniki.

- Visiting Hours: The site is generally open to visitors during daylight hours, with specific operating hours varying by season. It's advisable to check with local authorities or the Chalkidiki Tourism Organization for the most up-to-date information on visiting hours and admission fees.

Petralona Cave

- History: The Petralona Cave is a unique natural wonder with significant historical importance. It gained fame in 1960 when a skull of an ancient human, believed to be around 700,000 years old, was discovered within the cave. The cave has been a site of ongoing archaeological research and is known for its impressive stalactites and stalagmites.

- Location: The Petralona Cave is located near the village of Petralona in the eastern part of the Kassandra Peninsula. It's approximately 50 kilometers from Thessaloniki.

- Visiting Hours: The cave is open to the public and generally follows seasonal schedules. It's recommended to check with the cave's official website or the Petralona Archaeological Site for the latest information on visiting hours and ticket prices.

Athos Monastic Community

- History: The Athos Monastic Community, also known as Mount Athos, is a UNESCO World Heritage site and a unique monastic republic. It has a history dating back over a thousand years, with the first monastic communities established in the

9th century. Today, it remains a spiritual and cultural hub for Orthodox Christianity.

- Location: Mount Athos occupies the entire Athos Peninsula, the easternmost "leg" of Halkidiki. Access to the monastic community is restricted, and only males with special permits are allowed to visit. Boat tours that circumnavigate the peninsula offer breathtaking views of the monasteries and the surrounding landscape.

- Visiting Hours: While most of Mount Athos is not accessible to the public, visitors can take boat tours that offer views of the monasteries. These tours generally operate during the tourist season, and the exact schedules can vary. It's advisable to contact tour operators in advance for the most current information.

Nikiti Old Village

- History: Nikiti is one of the oldest settlements in Sithonia, dating back to the 14th century. The old village is characterized by its traditional architecture, cobblestone streets, and charming atmosphere. It's a glimpse into the region's history and a place where time seems to stand still.

- Location: Nikiti Old Village is located in Sithonia, the central "leg" of Halkidiki. It's a short drive from the modern coastal town of Nikiti.

- Visiting Hours: Nikiti Old Village is open to visitors year-round. Exploring the historic streets and buildings is a delightful experience, and there are no specific visiting hours or admission fees.

Sani Resort and Marina

- History: Sani Resort is a luxury resort complex that has become a renowned destination in Halkidiki. It offers a range of upscale accommodations, restaurants, and entertainment options. The marina at Sani Resort has played a vital role in promoting nautical tourism in the region.

- Location: Sani Resort is situated on the Kassandra Peninsula, Halkidiki. It's approximately 70 kilometers from Thessaloniki.

- Visiting Hours: Sani Resort and its marina are open year-round, with various facilities and restaurants operating based on seasonal schedules. You can contact the resort directly for information on visiting hours and reservations.

Turtle Lake

- History: Turtle Lake, known locally as "Gaidourorachi," is a small, idyllic lake surrounded by lush greenery. The lake is a natural habitat for several species of freshwater turtles and other wildlife. It's a peaceful spot to connect with nature and enjoy the outdoors.

- Location: Turtle Lake is located in Sithonia, not far from the village of Ormylia. It's nestled within a picturesque forested area, providing a tranquil escape.

- Visiting Hours: As a natural attraction, Turtle Lake doesn't have set visiting hours, and there are no admission fees. It's accessible year-round, and you can enjoy leisurely walks around the lake and the surrounding forest.

Each of these attractions in Halkidiki offers a unique glimpse into the region's history, natural beauty, and cultural heritage. Whether you're interested in archaeology, spirituality, or simply enjoying the serene landscapes, Halkidiki's must-see landmarks have something for every traveler to appreciate.

CHAPTER 5:

Embracing Halkidiki's Rich Culture

Halkidiki's culture is a vibrant tapestry woven from centuries of history, a deep connection to the land and sea, and a warm and welcoming spirit. In this chapter, we will delve into the rich cultural aspects of Halkidiki, including its gastronomic delights, traditional cuisine, festivals and celebrations, folklore, artisan crafts, and the music and dance that make Halkidiki a unique and culturally diverse destination.

Halkidiki's Gastronomy Delights

Halkidiki's gastronomy is a celebration of fresh, locally-sourced ingredients and a harmonious blend of Mediterranean flavors. With its proximity to the sea, you can expect seafood to play a prominent role in local dishes. Some culinary delights to savor in Halkidiki include:

- Fresh Seafood: From grilled octopus to succulent mussels and the catch of the day, Halkidiki's coastline offers an abundance of seafood. Try "psarosoupa," a traditional Greek fisherman's soup, for a taste of the sea.

- Olive Oil: Halkidiki is known for its olive groves, producing some of the finest olive oil in Greece. Sample local olives, olive oil, and dishes like "ladera," made with vegetables cooked in olive oil.

- Honey: The region's honey, often sourced from the nearby Mount Athos, is renowned for its quality. Taste traditional Greek pastries drizzled with local honey.

- Wine: Halkidiki is home to several wineries that produce excellent wines. Explore local vineyards and savor a glass of Assyrtiko or Xinomavro, two prominent Greek grape varieties.

- Bougatsa: Try the local pastry called "bougatsa," a sweet or savory treat made from thin layers of dough filled with cream, cheese, or other delicious fillings.

Traditional Chalkidian Cuisine

Chalkidian cuisine, with its roots deep in tradition, offers a rich array of dishes that reflect the region's cultural heritage. Some traditional Chalkidian dishes to seek out include:

- Choriatiki Salad: The classic Greek salad, featuring tomatoes, cucumbers, olives, onions, and feta cheese, often drizzled with local olive oil.

- Gyros: A beloved street food, gyros consists of sliced meat, usually pork or chicken, wrapped in pita bread and topped with tomatoes, onions, and tzatziki sauce.

- Soutzouk Loukoum: This sweet treat is a type of Turkish delight, made from sugar, starch, and a variety of flavorings such as rosewater and nuts.

- Tzatziki: A cooling dip made from yogurt, cucumbers, garlic, and dill, often served with bread or as a condiment for grilled meats.

- Mousaka: A baked casserole made from layers of eggplant, minced meat, and béchamel sauce.

- Koulouri: A ring-shaped bread roll covered in sesame seeds, perfect for a quick snack.

Festivals and Celebrations

Halkidiki comes alive with festivals and celebrations that showcase the region's rich cultural heritage and traditions. Some notable events to experience include:

- Assumption of the Virgin Mary: Celebrated on August 15th, this religious festival honors the Assumption of the Virgin Mary and is marked by church services and processions in many villages.

- Kassandra Festival: Held in the town of Kassandreia, this festival features a diverse program of cultural events, including music, dance, and theatrical performances.

- Kallithea Festival: Kallithea hosts a lively summer festival with live music, dance, and cultural exhibitions, creating a festive atmosphere for locals and visitors.

- Mount Athos Celebration: While visitors are generally not allowed on Mount Athos itself, you can join in the festivities surrounding the religious celebrations of the monastic community from a distance. The monasteries mark various saints' days with special church services and rituals.

Folklore and Artisan Crafts

Halkidiki's folklore and artisan crafts are deeply rooted in tradition and craftsmanship. Local artisans create a wide range of products, often by hand, including:

- Embroidery and Textiles: The region is known for its intricate embroidery work, which adorns clothing, table linens, and more.

- Ceramics: Halkidiki's potters create beautiful ceramics, from functional pieces like plates and mugs to decorative items.

- Traditional Jewelry: Look for unique jewelry pieces that reflect the traditional style of the region, often featuring intricate metalwork and semi-precious stones.

- Icons and Religious Art: Given the strong religious influence in Halkidiki, you can find icons and religious artwork that make for meaningful souvenirs.

- Woodcraft: Local woodcraft includes items like hand-carved furniture, utensils, and decorative pieces, often showcasing intricate designs.

Local Music and Dance

Music and dance are integral to Halkidiki's cultural fabric. Local festivals and events often feature traditional Greek music and dance performances. The region's musical heritage includes genres like "rembetika," which tell stories of daily life through song, as well as lively Greek folk music.

Don't be surprised if you find yourself joining in on a spontaneous dance at a local taverna or festival. Greek dance is a communal activity that brings people together in celebration.

Embracing Halkidiki's rich culture means savoring the flavors of its cuisine, admiring traditional crafts, and participating in the region's vibrant festivals and traditions. The warm hospitality and strong ties to tradition make Halkidiki a place where you can truly immerse yourself in Greek culture.

CHAPTER 6:

Outdoor Adventures and Recreational Activities

Halkidiki's diverse landscapes and Mediterranean climate create the perfect backdrop for a wide range of outdoor adventures and recreational activities. In this chapter, we'll explore the various ways you can enjoy the natural beauty and outdoor experiences that Halkidiki has to offer, including hiking in the region's forests, indulging in watersports and beach activities, embarking on cruises in the Aegean Sea, birdwatching in Axios Delta National Park, golfing in Halkidiki, and taking day trips to nearby islands.

Hiking in Halkidiki's Forests

Halkidiki's lush forests, rolling hills, and scenic trails offer fantastic opportunities for hikers of all levels. Here are some popular hiking destinations:

- Holomontas Mountain: This mountain range in central Halkidiki offers a network of trails that wind through pine forests and lead to panoramic viewpoints. The trails range from easy to challenging, making it suitable for hikers of various skill levels.

- Sithonia Peninsula: Sithonia is home to a variety of hiking paths that meander through picturesque landscapes. The coastline trail offers stunning sea views, while the wooded interior provides a peaceful retreat.

- Itamos Mountain: Located in the Kassandra Peninsula, Itamos Mountain is a serene area with well-marked hiking trails. The paths lead through pine forests and to secluded beaches, where you can take a refreshing dip.

- Kallithea - Kriopigi Trail: This coastal trail on the Kassandra Peninsula offers a mix of forested paths and seaside walks, providing a perfect blend of nature and beautiful beaches.

Whether you're an experienced hiker seeking a challenge or a casual stroller looking for a leisurely nature walk, Halkidiki's hiking options will connect you with the region's natural beauty.

Watersports and Beach Activities

Halkidiki's pristine beaches and crystal-clear waters make it an ideal destination for watersports and beach activities. The Mediterranean climate ensures that the sea is inviting throughout the summer. Some popular beach activities and watersports include:

- Swimming: With its numerous Blue Flag beaches, Halkidiki offers a wealth of options for a refreshing swim in the Aegean Sea.

- Snorkeling and Diving: The region's underwater world is a delight for snorkelers and divers. Discover vibrant marine life, shipwrecks, and underwater caves.

- Windsurfing and Kitesurfing: The windy conditions in some areas of Halkidiki, such as Kassandra, attract windsurfers and kitesurfers seeking thrilling experiences on the water.

- Jet Skiing and Parasailing: For adrenaline seekers, jet skiing and parasailing are popular activities offered at various beach resorts.

- Boating: Rent a boat or join a boat tour to explore hidden coves, secluded beaches, and nearby islands.

- Beach Volleyball: Many beach bars and resorts offer beach volleyball courts for some active fun in the sun.

- Beach Yoga: Experience the serenity of beach yoga sessions offered at some resorts and wellness centers.

Cruising the Aegean Sea

Exploring Halkidiki's coastline by boat is an enchanting experience. Whether you opt for a full-day cruise or a shorter excursion, you'll be treated to breathtaking views, hidden coves, and a taste of local culture. Some of the popular boat trips and cruises include:

- Mount Athos Cruises: These cruises take you along the coastline of Mount Athos, allowing you to view the monastic community and its monasteries from the sea.

- Sithonia Peninsula Cruises: Explore the pristine beaches and bays of Sithonia on a boat tour. You'll have the chance to swim in secluded coves and enjoy a leisurely day at sea.

- Sunset Cruises: Evening cruises provide a romantic setting to enjoy the sunset while savoring a delicious dinner on board.

- Boat Parties: Some operators offer lively boat parties with music, dancing, and entertainment, creating a festive atmosphere.

- Fishing Tours: If you're a fishing enthusiast, consider joining a fishing tour to try your hand at catching local fish.

Bird Watching in Axios Delta National Park

Axios Delta National Park, situated in the Thessaloniki region near Halkidiki, is a paradise for birdwatchers and nature enthusiasts. This wetland area is home to over 300 bird species, making it one of the most important bird habitats in Greece. Visitors can spot flamingos, herons, cormorants, and various other waterfowl. There are observation points, walking trails, and guided tours available to enhance your birdwatching experience.

Golfing in Halkidiki

For golf enthusiasts, Halkidiki offers several golf courses set in stunning natural surroundings. Some of the golf courses in the region include:

- Porto Carras Golf Club: Located in Sithonia, this 18-hole golf course offers challenging play and beautiful sea views.

- Sani Golf Club: Situated in the Kassandra Peninsula, Sani Golf Club provides golfers with a well-designed course surrounded by nature.

- Gerakini Golf Club: A short drive from Halkidiki, this course is popular for its picturesque location and serene atmosphere.

Day Trips to Nearby Islands

Halkidiki's strategic location on the Aegean Sea makes it an excellent starting point for day trips to nearby islands. Some islands within easy reach of Halkidiki include:

- Diaporos Island: Located in the Vourvourou area of Sithonia, Diaporos is known for its crystal-clear waters and hidden coves. You can rent a boat and explore this idyllic island at your own pace.

- Amouliani Island: A short ferry ride from the Ouranoupoli port takes you to Amouliani, the only inhabited island in Halkidiki. Enjoy its pristine beaches and authentic Greek atmosphere.

- Thassos Island: Although a bit farther from Halkidiki, Thassos is accessible by ferry and makes for a wonderful day trip. Explore its charming villages, ancient ruins, and beautiful beaches.

- Kassandra Peninsula: If you're staying on one of Halkidiki's peninsulas, consider exploring the neighboring peninsulas for a day. Take a scenic drive along the coast, stop at beaches and villages, and savor the local cuisine.

Halkidiki's outdoor adventures and recreational activities offer a dynamic way to experience the region's natural beauty, from hiking in its forests to watersports on its pristine beaches, cruising the Aegean Sea, birdwatching in Axios Delta National Park, golfing on scenic courses, and embarking on exciting day trips to nearby islands. Whether you seek thrilling experiences or tranquil moments in nature, Halkidiki has something for every outdoor enthusiast.

CHAPTER 7:

Halkidiki for All Travelers

Halkidiki is a destination that caters to a diverse range of travelers, ensuring that everyone, from families to couples, seniors, students, and solo adventurers, can find their own piece of paradise. In this chapter, we will explore the offerings and experiences that Halkidiki provides for each category of traveler, ensuring that your visit to this Greek gem is tailor-made to your preferences.

Family-Friendly Experiences

Halkidiki is a fantastic destination for family vacations, offering a wide array of family-friendly experiences and amenities:

- Blue Flag Beaches: Many of Halkidiki's beaches proudly bear the Blue Flag certification, indicating clean, safe, and well-maintained shores ideal for families.

- Water Parks: Family-friendly water parks, like Waterland in Thessaloniki, offer thrilling rides and aquatic fun for all ages.

- Outdoor Adventures: Families can explore nature together, hiking through forests, enjoying beach days, or taking boat trips to discover hidden coves and islands.

- Cultural Exploration: Delve into the region's history with visits to archaeological sites and monasteries, making for educational and enjoyable excursions.

- Kid-Friendly Dining: Many restaurants in Halkidiki offer child-friendly menus and warm hospitality for families.

- Resort Amenities: Numerous resorts and hotels cater to families, providing kids' clubs, entertainment, and childcare services.

- Safety: Halkidiki is known for its overall safety, making it a worry-free destination for families.

Romantic Escapes for Couples

Halkidiki offers a romantic ambiance that's perfect for couples seeking intimate experiences:

- Sunset Dinners: Enjoy romantic sunset dinners at beachfront restaurants or on a cruise, with breathtaking views of the Aegean Sea.

- Private Beaches: Many hotels and resorts have their own private beaches, allowing couples to relax in solitude.

- Couples' Spas: Experience relaxing massages and spa treatments together at world-class wellness centers.

- Wine Tasting: Savor Greek wines on vineyard tours and tastings, a delightful way to spend quality time together.

- Beach Walks: Stroll along the sandy shores, hand in hand, under the moonlight, or explore secluded beaches only accessible by boat.

- Greece's Second Honeymoon: Halkidiki has become a destination for couples celebrating second honeymoons or special anniversaries, offering unforgettable moments.

- Privacy: Enjoy a sense of privacy and seclusion in boutique hotels, luxury resorts, and private villas.

Seniors' Relaxation Retreats

Halkidiki is an excellent choice for seniors looking to unwind, immerse themselves in nature, and savor the region's tranquility:

- Thermal Springs: Visit the thermal springs of Agia Paraskevi for therapeutic baths, relaxation, and rejuvenation.

- Nature Walks: Hike or walk through the serene landscapes, enjoying the slower pace and taking in the region's beauty.

- Village Life: Explore traditional villages and enjoy a glimpse into Greek village culture and hospitality.

- Mediterranean Diet: Savor the health benefits of the Mediterranean diet, with fresh, locally sourced ingredients.

- Peaceful Beaches: Relax on uncrowded beaches where the only sound is the gentle lapping of waves.

- Health and Wellness Retreats: Numerous resorts and wellness centers offer programs focused on health, relaxation, and rejuvenation.

- Cultural Exploration: Delve into the region's history through visits to archaeological sites, monasteries, and museums.

Halkidiki for Students

Halkidiki is a fantastic destination for students, offering a blend of relaxation and adventure:

- Affordability: Compared to some other European destinations, Halkidiki is budget-friendly, making it ideal for student travelers.

- Beach Parties: Join beach parties and nightlife in popular destinations like Kassandra, with a vibrant atmosphere and diverse music.

- Adventures: Enjoy thrilling water sports, hikes, and outdoor activities, perfect for active students.

- Local Cuisine: Savor Greek street food and local dishes for an authentic culinary experience.

- Nightlife: Thessaloniki, located near Halkidiki, is known for its vibrant nightlife, with plenty of bars, clubs, and live music venues.

- Cultural Exploration: Students can explore the rich history and cultural heritage of the region.

Solo Traveler's Guide and Safety Tips

Halkidiki is a welcoming destination for solo travelers, offering a mix of adventure and relaxation. Safety is a key concern for solo travelers, and Halkidiki is known for its overall safety. However, here are some additional safety tips:

- Accommodation: Choose reputable accommodations in well-visited areas. Many hotels have 24/7 front desks for assistance.

- Local Customs: Familiarize yourself with local customs and traditions to respect the culture.

- Emergency Contacts: Keep emergency contact numbers and the contact information of your country's embassy or consulate on hand.

- Travel Insurance: Purchase comprehensive travel insurance for peace of mind in case of unexpected events.

- Solo Activities: Engage in group tours and activities to meet other travelers and reduce isolation.

- Local Transportation: Familiarize yourself with local transportation options and schedules. Taxis and rideshare apps are readily available.

- Language: While English is widely spoken, learning a few basic Greek phrases can be useful and appreciated by locals.

- Exploration: Halkidiki is a safe destination for exploring on your own, but always let someone know your plans and expected return time when heading out for adventures.

Halkidiki welcomes all types of travelers, ensuring that families, couples, seniors, students, and solo adventurers can enjoy their visit to the fullest. With a wide array of experiences and a reputation for safety, Halkidiki is the ideal Greek destination for everyone.

CHAPTER 8:

Practical Information and Resources

This chapter provides essential practical information and resources to help you make the most of your trip to Halkidiki. From currency and language to health and safety guidelines, sustainable travel, and emergency contacts, here's everything you need to know before you go.

Currency and Money Matters

- Currency: The official currency of Greece is the Euro (€). ATMs are widely available in Halkidiki, and credit cards are accepted at most hotels, restaurants, and shops. Traveler's checks are generally not widely used.

- Currency Exchange: You can exchange foreign currency for Euros at local banks, exchange offices, and some hotels. However, using ATMs for currency withdrawal is usually more convenient and provides competitive exchange rates.

- Tipping: Tipping is customary in Halkidiki, with 10% to 15% being the usual tip at restaurants. In bars and cafes, rounding up the bill is common. Taxi drivers and hotel staff also appreciate small tips for their services.

Language and Communication

- Language: Greek is the official language in Halkidiki. While many locals in the tourist areas speak English and other foreign languages, learning a few basic Greek phrases can be a helpful and appreciated gesture.

- Communication: Halkidiki has good mobile network coverage, and you can easily get a local SIM card for your phone. International roaming services are also available for travelers who prefer to use their home number.

Health and Safety Guidelines

- Healthcare: Halkidiki has modern medical facilities and pharmacies. European Union citizens can receive medical treatment through the European Health Insurance Card (EHIC). Travelers from non-EU countries should have comprehensive travel insurance covering medical expenses.

- Travel Insurance: It is advisable to have comprehensive travel insurance that includes coverage for medical emergencies, trip cancellations, and other unforeseen events.

- Safety: Halkidiki is generally a safe destination for travelers. However, it's wise to take standard safety precautions, such as safeguarding your belongings, staying in well-lit areas at night, and avoiding risky activities.

- Sun Protection: The Mediterranean sun can be intense. Make sure to use sunscreen, wear a hat, and stay hydrated, especially during the summer months.

- Emergency Services: In case of emergency, dial 112 for general emergencies, including medical assistance, police, and fire services.

Sustainable Travel in Halkidiki

Halkidiki is dedicated to promoting sustainable travel and responsible tourism. You can contribute to preserving the natural beauty and culture of the region by following these guidelines:

- Respect Nature: Stay on marked paths when hiking, and don't disturb local wildlife. Avoid littering and leave no trace of your visit.

- Reduce Plastic Use: Use reusable water bottles and bags to minimize plastic waste. Many businesses are transitioning to eco-friendly practices.

- Support Local: Choose locally-owned accommodations, restaurants, and shops to support the local economy and culture.

- Conserve Resources: Save water and energy in your accommodation by following their eco-friendly policies.

- Cultural Sensitivity: Respect local customs and traditions, including appropriate attire when visiting religious sites.

- Reduce Carbon Emissions: Use public transportation or carpooling, and consider eco-friendly activities like cycling and hiking.

Emergency Contacts and Useful Information

Emergency Services: In case of an emergency, here are some important contact numbers:

- Police: 100
- Fire Department: 199
- Medical Emergency: 112
- Tourist Police: +30 2310 575 770

- Embassies and Consulates: If you need assistance from your country's embassy or consulate, here are some of them in Greece:

- Embassy of the United States, Athens: +30 210 721 2951
- Embassy of the United Kingdom, Athens: +30 210 7272 600
- Embassy of Canada, Athens: +30 210 727 3400

Tourist Information: Halkidiki has tourist information centers where you can get maps, brochures, and local advice:

- Halkidiki Tourism Organization: +30 2371 350 900
- Halkidiki Tourist Police: +30 2310 575 770

Embassies and consulate contact details may change, so it's essential to verify the current information on the official websites of your country's diplomatic mission. Additionally, keep in mind that Halkidiki has different peninsulas, each with its own unique attractions and character. Research and plan your trip accordingly to make the most of your visit to this beautiful region.

APPENDIX I:

Essential Travel Resources for Halkidiki

This appendix provides a collection of essential travel resources to help you plan and navigate your journey through Halkidiki. From travel apps and checklists to banking and currency exchange information, these resources will assist you in making your trip as smooth and enjoyable as possible.

Greek Phrases for Travelers with Pronunciation Guide

Basic Phrases for Greek Travel

1. Hello / Hi: Γειά σας (Yia sas)
2. Good morning: Καλημέρα (Kalimera)
3. Good afternoon: Καλησπέρα (Kalispera)

4. Good evening: Καληνύχτα (Kalinichta)

5. Please: Παρακαλώ (Parakalo)

6. Thank you: Ευχαριστώ (Efharisto)

7. Yes: Ναι (Ne)

8. No: Όχι (Ochi)

9. Excuse me / Sorry: Συγγνώμη (Signomi)

10. I don't understand: Δεν καταλαβαίνω (Den kataiaveno)

11. Help: Βοήθεια (Voithia)

12. How much is this?: Πόσο κοστίζει αυτό; (Poso kostizei afto?)

13. Where is the restroom?: Πού είναι η τουαλέτα; (Pou ine i tualeta?)

14. I need a doctor: Χρειάζομαι ένα γιατρό (Hriazome ena yatro)

Ordering Food and Drinks

1. Menu: Μενού (Menu)

2. Water: Νερό (Nero)

3. Coffee: Καφές (Kafes)

4. Tea: Τσάι (Tsai)

5. Beer: Μπύρα (Bira)

6. Wine: Κρασί (Krasi)

7. Bread: Ψωμί (Psomi)

8. Salt: Αλάτι (Alati)

9. Pepper: Πιπέρι (Piperi)

10. I'm a vegetarian: Είμαι χορτοφάγος (Eime chortofagos)

11. The check, please: Τον λογαριασμό, παρακαλώ (Ton logariasmo, parakalo)

12. I would like to order...: Θα ήθελα να παραγγείλω... (Tha ithela na paragilo...)

13. A table for [number] people: Ένα τραπέζι για [αριθμός] άτομα (Ena trapezi ya [arithmos] atoma)

Navigating Local Transportation

1. Bus: Λεωφορείο (Leoforeio)
2. Train: Τρένο (Treno)
3. Taxi: Ταξί (Taksi)
4. Airport: Αεροδρόμιο (Aerodromio)
5. Train station: Σταθμός τρένων (Stathmos treno)
6. Bus station: Σταθμός λεωφορείων (Stathmos leoforeion)
7. How much is a ticket to [destination]?: Πόσο κοστίζει ένα εισιτήριο για [προορισμός]; (Poso kostizei ena isitirio ya [proorismos]?)
8. Where is the nearest metro station?: Πού είναι ο πλησιέστερος σταθμός μετρό; (Pou ine o plisieros stathmos metro?)
9. I need a one-way/round-trip ticket: Χρειάζομαι ένα εισιτήριο (μονός/με επιστροφή); (Hriazome ena isitirio (monos/me epistrofi)?)

10. Is this the right bus/train for [destination]?: Είναι αυτό το σωστό λεωφορείο/τρένο για τον [προορισμό]; (Ine afto to sosto leoforeio/treno ya ton [proorismos]?)

Feel free to use these phrases during your travel to Greece to enhance your communication and cultural experience. The locals will appreciate your efforts to speak their language, even if it's just a few words

Recommended Travel Apps

1. Maps.me: This offline map app allows you to navigate Halkidiki without an internet connection. Download the Halkidiki map for easy access to directions and locations.

2. Halkidiki Guide: This mobile app offers detailed information on attractions, restaurants, hotels, and

activities in Halkidiki. It's an excellent companion for exploring the region.

3. XE Currency Converter: Keep track of currency exchange rates and convert your home currency to Euros while traveling in Halkidiki.

4. Google Translate: For non-Greek speakers, Google Translate is a valuable tool to help bridge language barriers.

5. Weather Apps: Download a weather app like Weather.com or AccuWeather to stay updated on local weather conditions, especially if you plan to spend time on the beach or outdoors.

6. Google Maps: While you'll need an internet connection for real-time navigation, Google Maps is an

excellent tool for finding nearby restaurants, attractions, and points of interest.

7. Halkidiki Public Transport: If you plan to use public transportation in Halkidiki, check if there's an official app for bus schedules and routes.

Other Useful Information

Halkidiki Travel Checklist

Before embarking on your trip to Halkidiki, consider this travel checklist to ensure you have all the essentials in order:

- Valid passport (with at least six months validity beyond your planned departure date)
- Visa (if required for your nationality)

- Travel insurance (covering medical emergencies, trip cancellations, and other unforeseen events)
- Accommodation reservations (including contact details)
- Flight tickets and itinerary
- Travel adapters and chargers for your electronic devices
- Essential medications and prescriptions (with copies)
- Copies of important documents (passport, travel insurance, driver's license, etc.)
- Local currency (Euros) and a small amount of cash for immediate expenses
- Credit cards and debit cards (inform your bank of your travel plans)
- Mobile phone and charger
- Travel guides and maps
- Travel-sized toiletries and personal hygiene items
- Comfortable walking shoes and appropriate clothing for the season

- Necessary travel accessories (e.g., sunglasses, sunblock, hats, and beach towels)

- Emergency contact information (for embassies/consulates and loved ones)

- Local emergency contact numbers (police, medical, fire, tourist police)

Banking and Currency Exchange Information

- Currency: The official currency of Greece is the Euro (€). Halkidiki has numerous ATMs, and credit cards are widely accepted in hotels, restaurants, and shops.

- ATMs: Automated Teller Machines (ATMs) are accessible throughout Halkidiki, allowing you to withdraw cash in Euros. Most ATMs provide instructions in multiple languages, making it easy for international travelers to use them.

- Currency Exchange: You can exchange foreign currency for Euros at local banks, exchange offices, and some hotels. However, it's often more convenient and cost-effective to use ATMs for currency withdrawal.

- Banks: Greek banks typically operate from 8:00 AM to 2:30 PM on weekdays, and some have extended hours. Currency exchange services are also available at banks.

- Credit Cards: Most major credit cards, including Visa, MasterCard, and American Express, are accepted at hotels, restaurants, and larger stores. Inform your bank of your travel plans to avoid any card issues.

- Traveler's Checks: Traveler's checks are not widely used in Halkidiki, and it's advisable to carry Euros for daily expenses.
- Currency Exchange Rates: Currency exchange rates can fluctuate, so it's a good idea to check rates at multiple locations before making an exchange. Banks generally offer competitive rates.

Remember to keep a record of your card details and the local contact numbers for your bank in case of any issues with your cards. Always exercise caution when using ATMs and ensure you're in a well-lit, secure location. Additionally, consider carrying a small amount of cash for immediate expenses upon arrival in Halkidiki.

Halkidiki Travel Guide 2024...

APPENDIX II:

Map of Halkidiki

✈ TRAVEL ITINERARY

Destination:	Duration:
Arrival:	Departure:

Hotel Address:
Transportation:

Day 1

Time	Activity
8:00 am	
12:00 nn	
1:00 pm	
3:00 pm	
7:00 pm	
10:00 pm	

Day 2

Time	Activity
8:00 am	
12:00 nn	
1:00 pm	
3:00 pm	
7:00 pm	
10:00 pm	

Day 3

Time	Activity
8:00 am	
12:00 nn	
1:00 pm	
3:00 pm	
7:00 pm	
10:00 pm	

TRAVEL

DATE:
DURATION:

DESTINATION:

PLACES TO SEE:
1.
2.
3.
4.
5.
6.
7.

LOCAL FOOD TO TRY:
1.
2.
3.
4.
5.
6.
7.

DAY 1

DAY 2

DAY 3

DAY 4

DAY 5

DAY 6

NOTES

EXPENSES IN TOTAL:

PLANNER

GENERAL NOTE

Printed in Great Britain
by Amazon